SAYINGS & EXPRESSIONS
STAINED GLASS PATTERNS

ANNA CROYLE

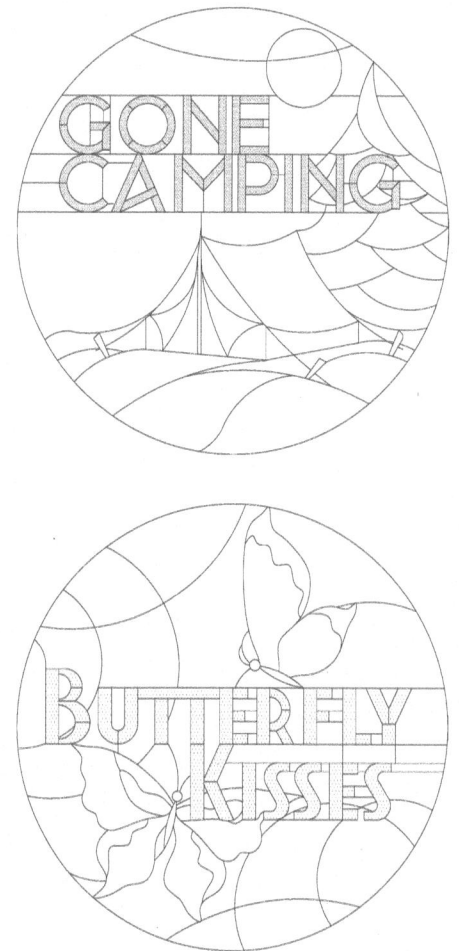

DOVER PUBLICATIONS, INC., MINEOLA, NEW YORK

Bibliographical Note

Sayings & Expressions: Stained Glass Patterns is a new work,
first published by Dover Publications, Inc., in 2020.

Library of Congress Cataloging-in-Publication Data

Names: Croyle, Anna, author.
Title: Sayings & expressions: stained glass patterns / Anna Croyle.
Other titles: Sayings and expressions
Description: Mineola, New York: Dover Publications, Inc., 2020.
Identifiers: LCCN 2019056125 | ISBN 9780486842165
Subjects: LCSH: Glass craft—Patterns. | Glass painting and Staining—Patterns. |
   Aphorisms and apothegms.
Classification: LCC TT298 .C766 2020 | DDC 748.5028—dc23
LC record available at https://lccn.loc.gov/2019056125

Manufactured in the United States of America
84216902
www.doverpublications.com

Inspirational sayings highlight the 40 contemporary designs in this stunning collection of patterns for use in your next stained glass project. Artist Anna Croyle has provided a beautiful variety of black-and-white template patterns that may be reproduced in smaller or larger sizes for any number of projects. Also provided are two different styles of alphabets and numbers for your own personalization.

If you're new to stained glass crafting, we suggest you supplement this book with an instruction book such as *Stained Glass Craft Made Simple* by James McDonell, Dover Publications, Inc., 978-0-486-24963-6. All materials needed, including general instructions and tools for beginners, can be purchased from local craft or hobby stores, or on the Internet.

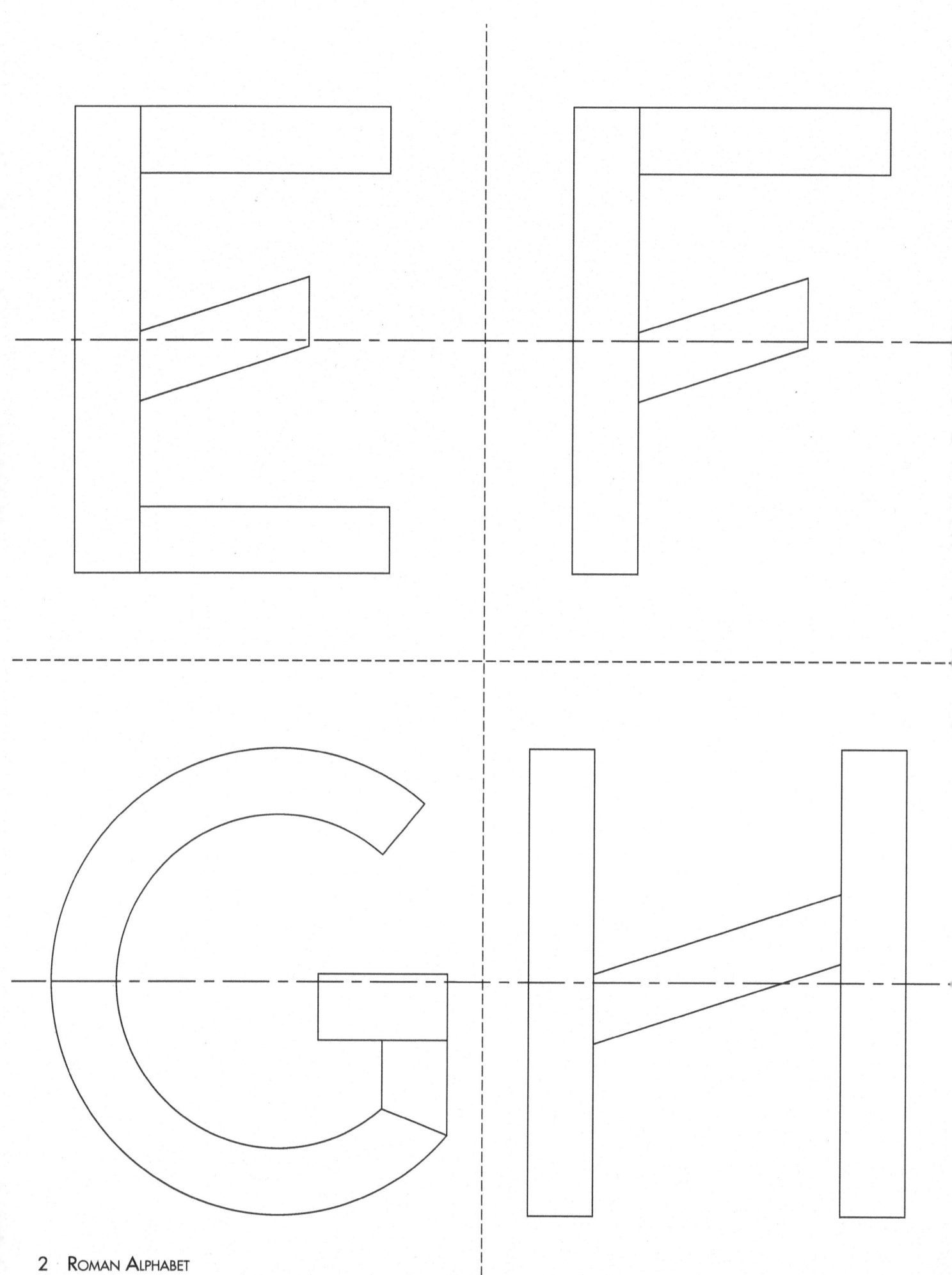

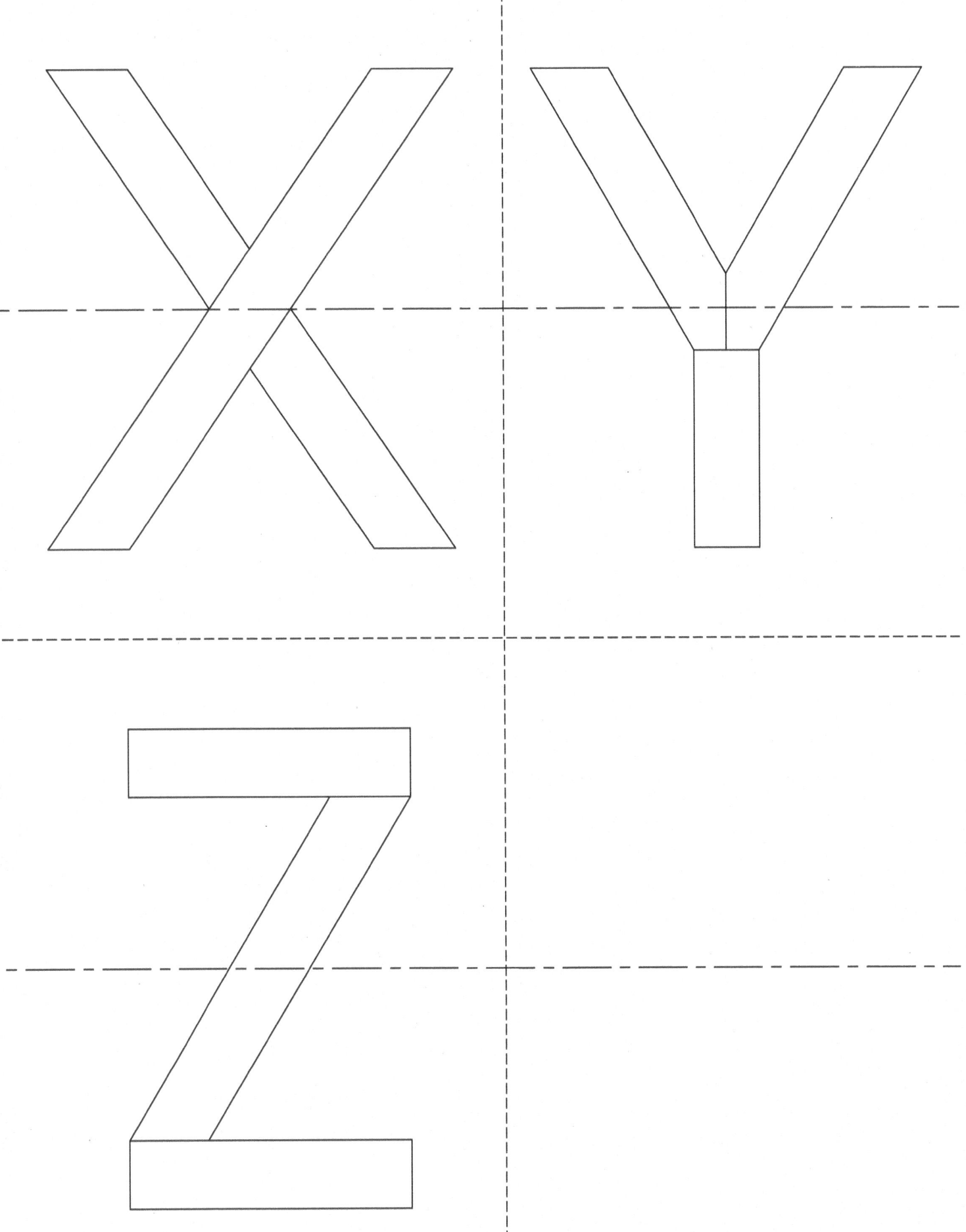

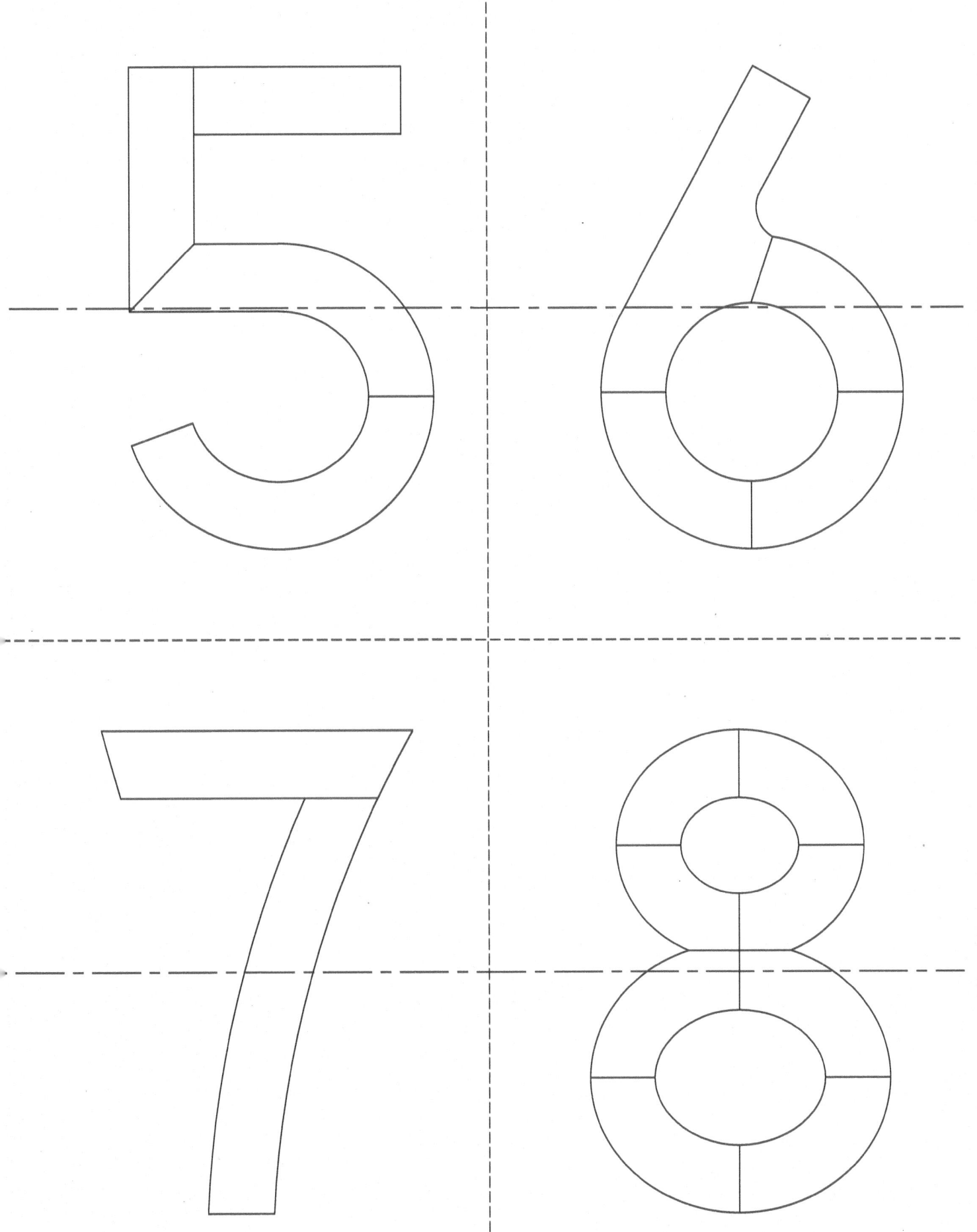

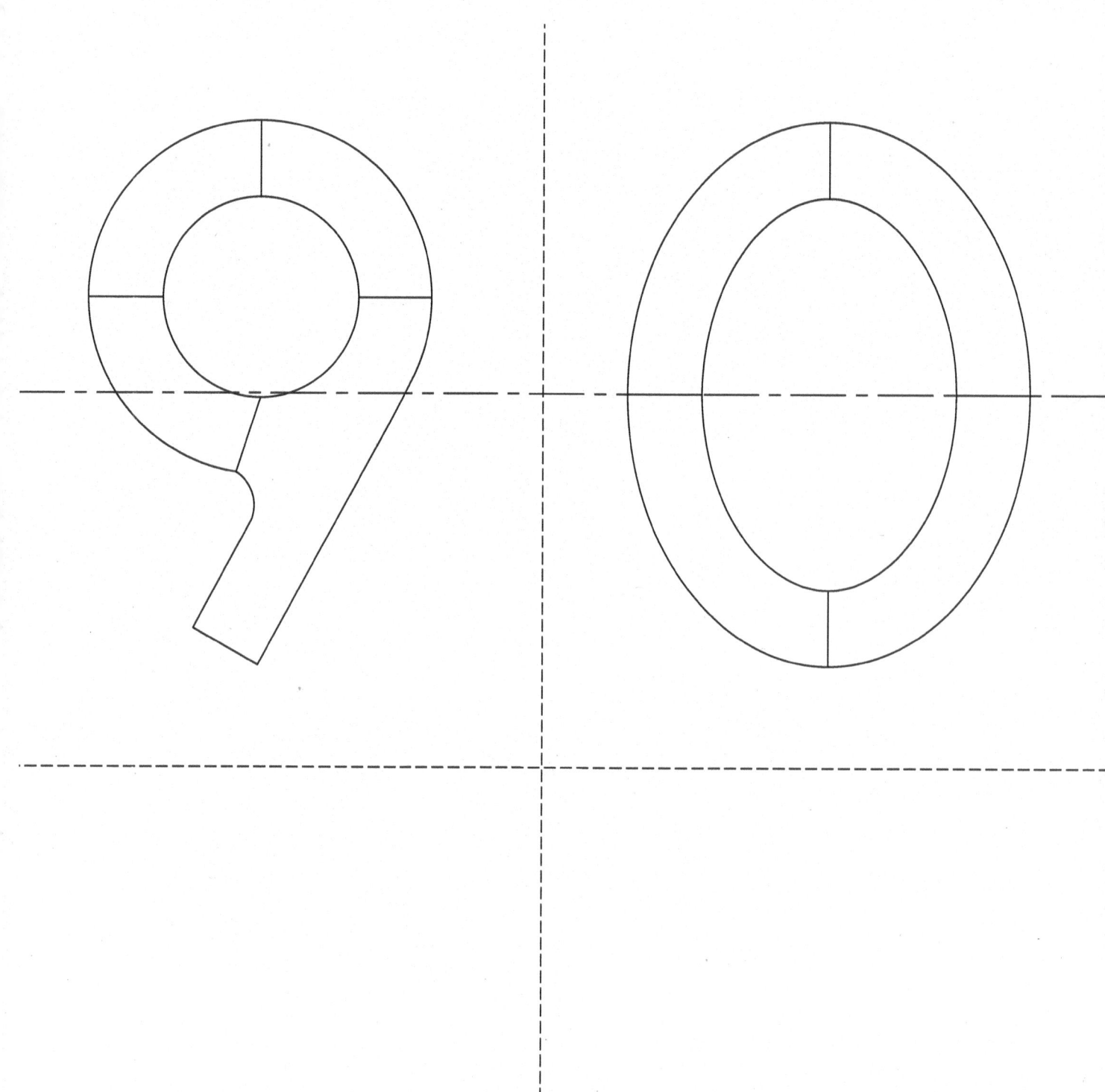

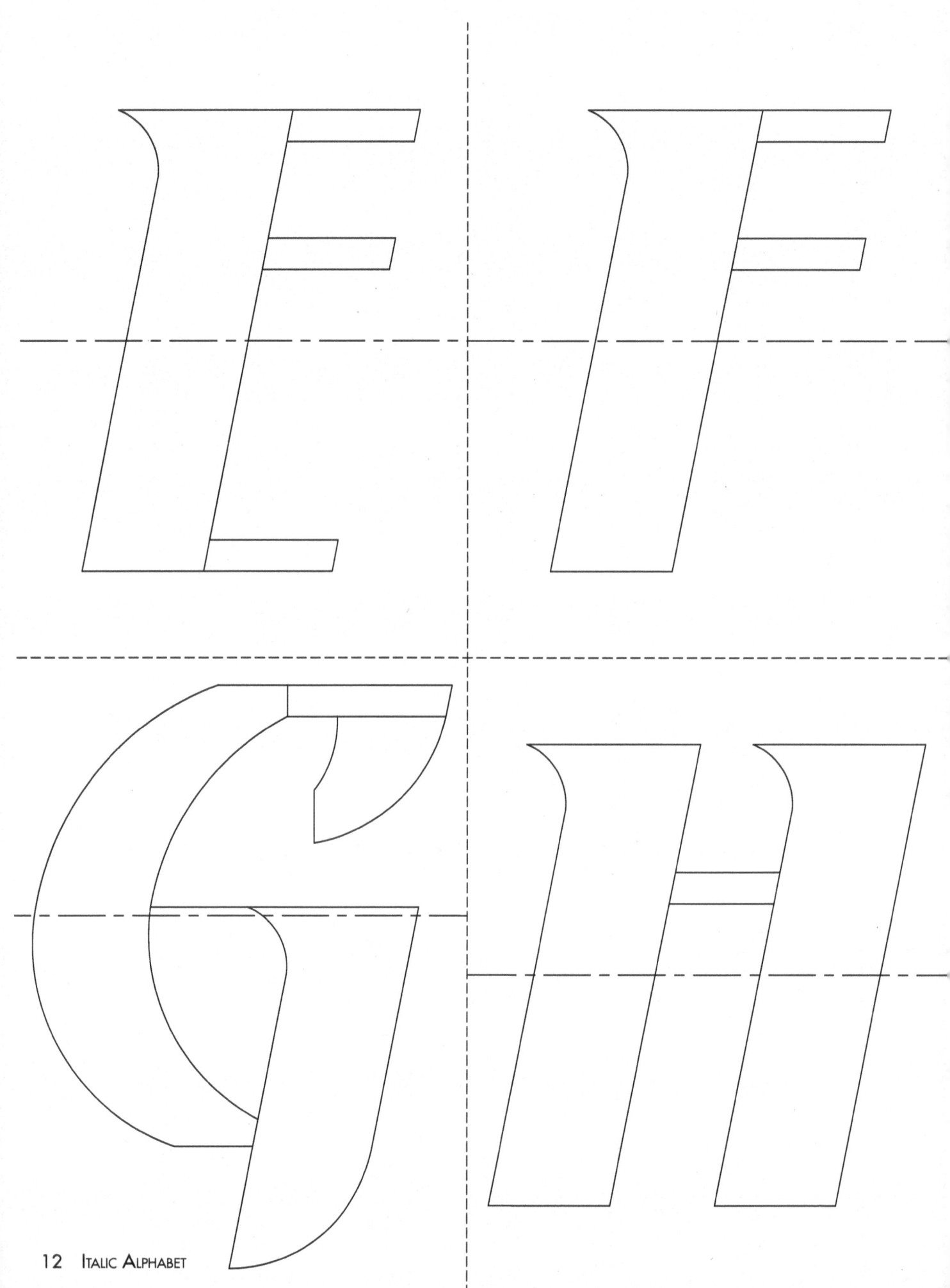

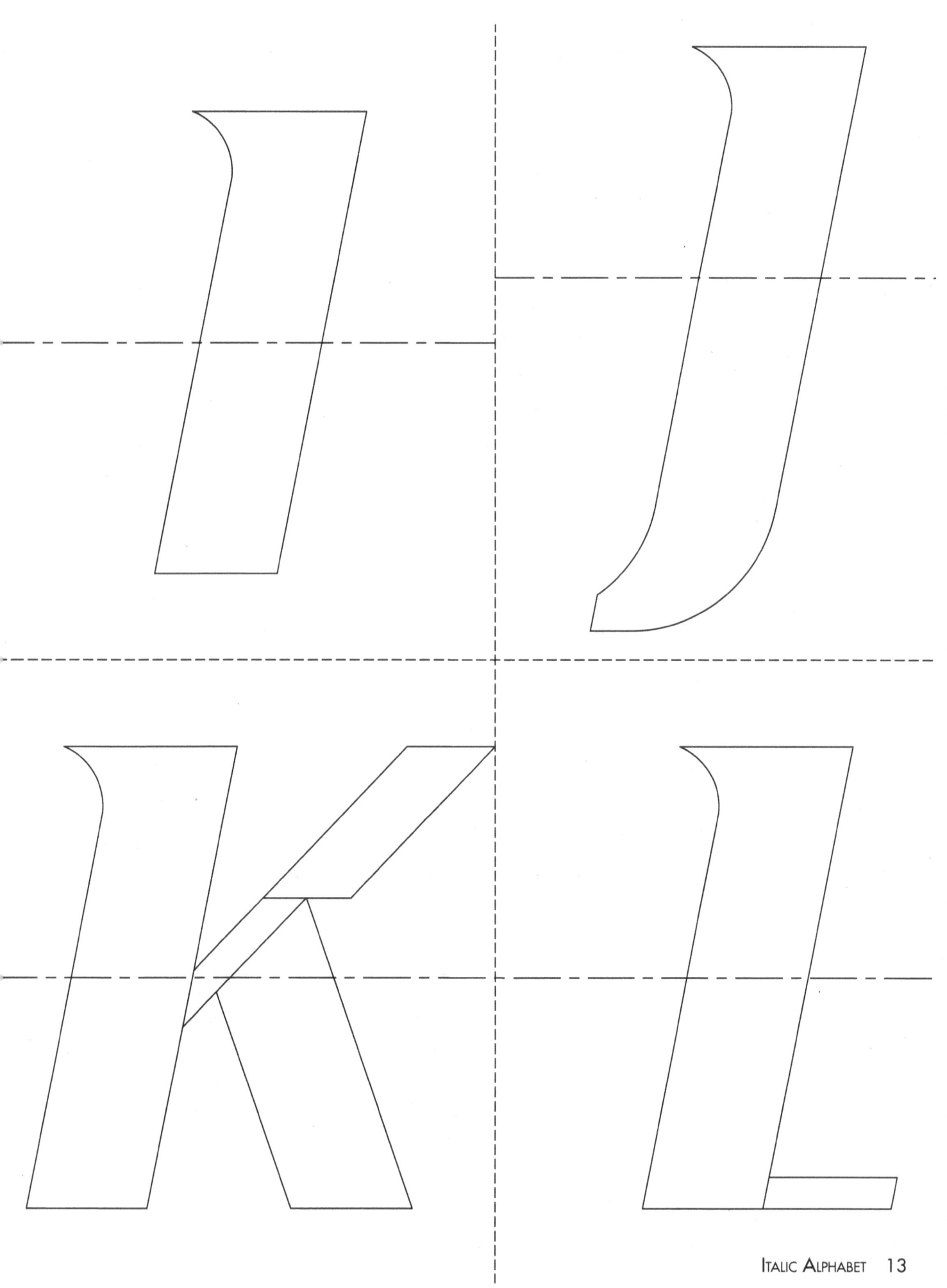

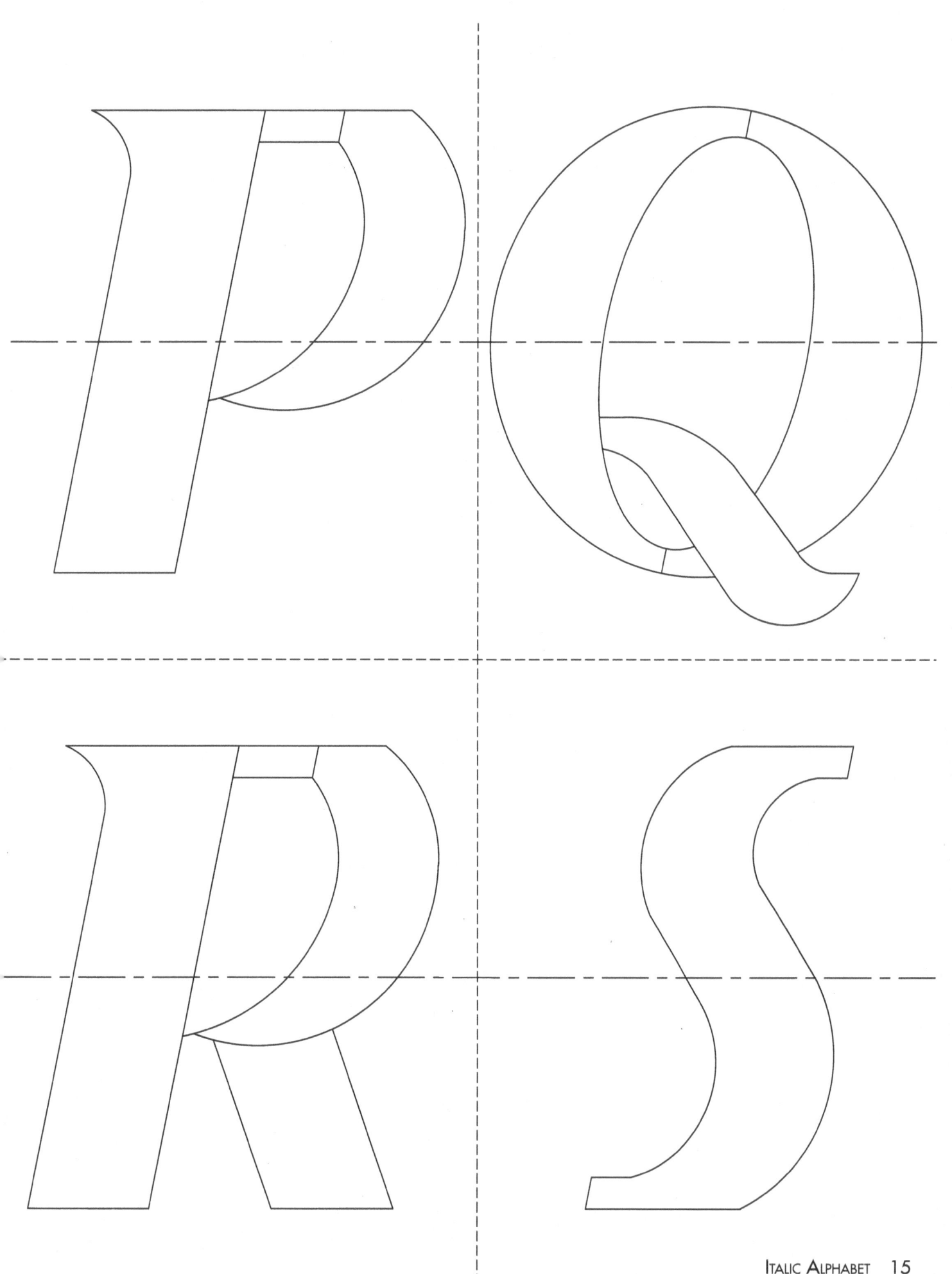

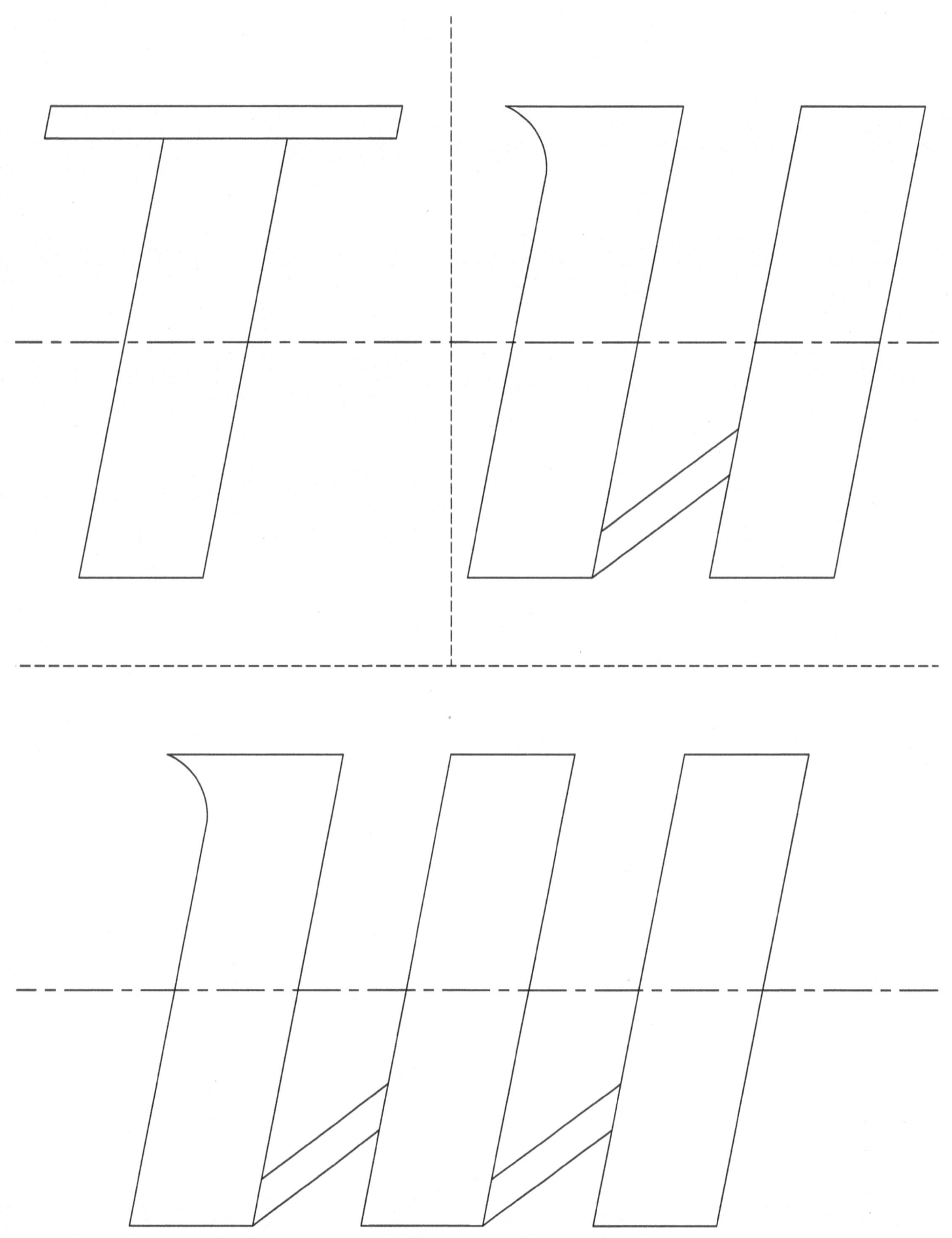

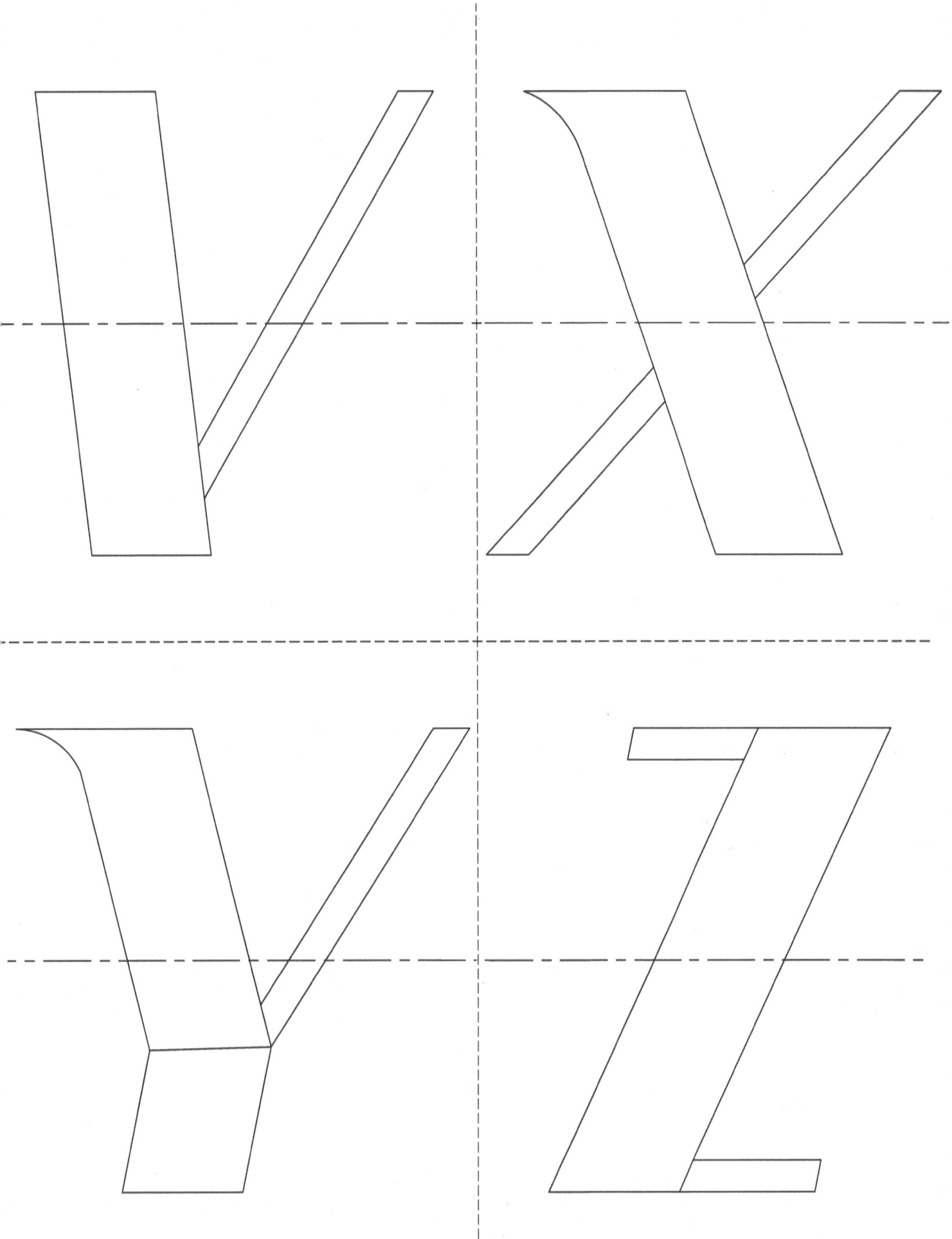

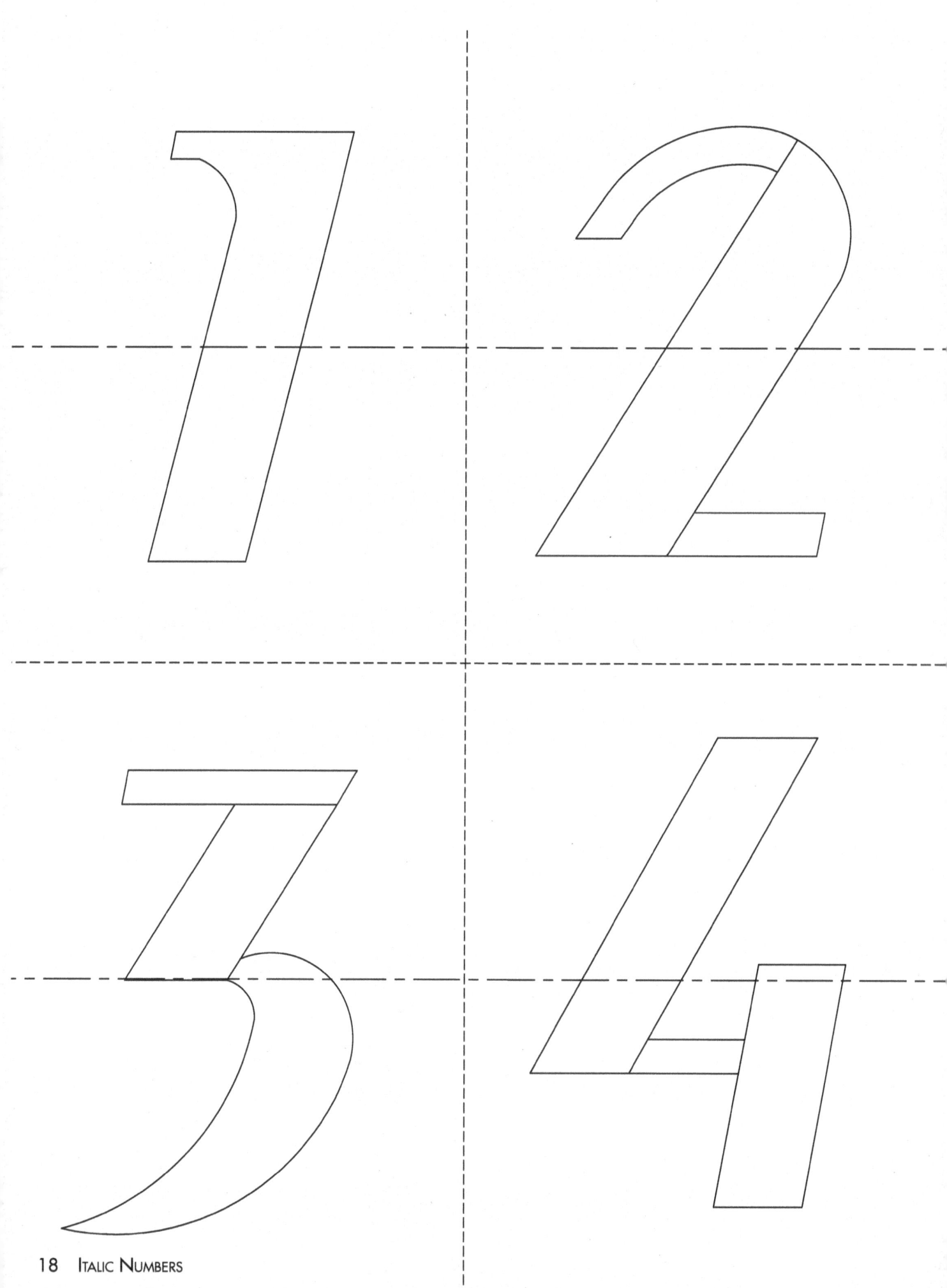

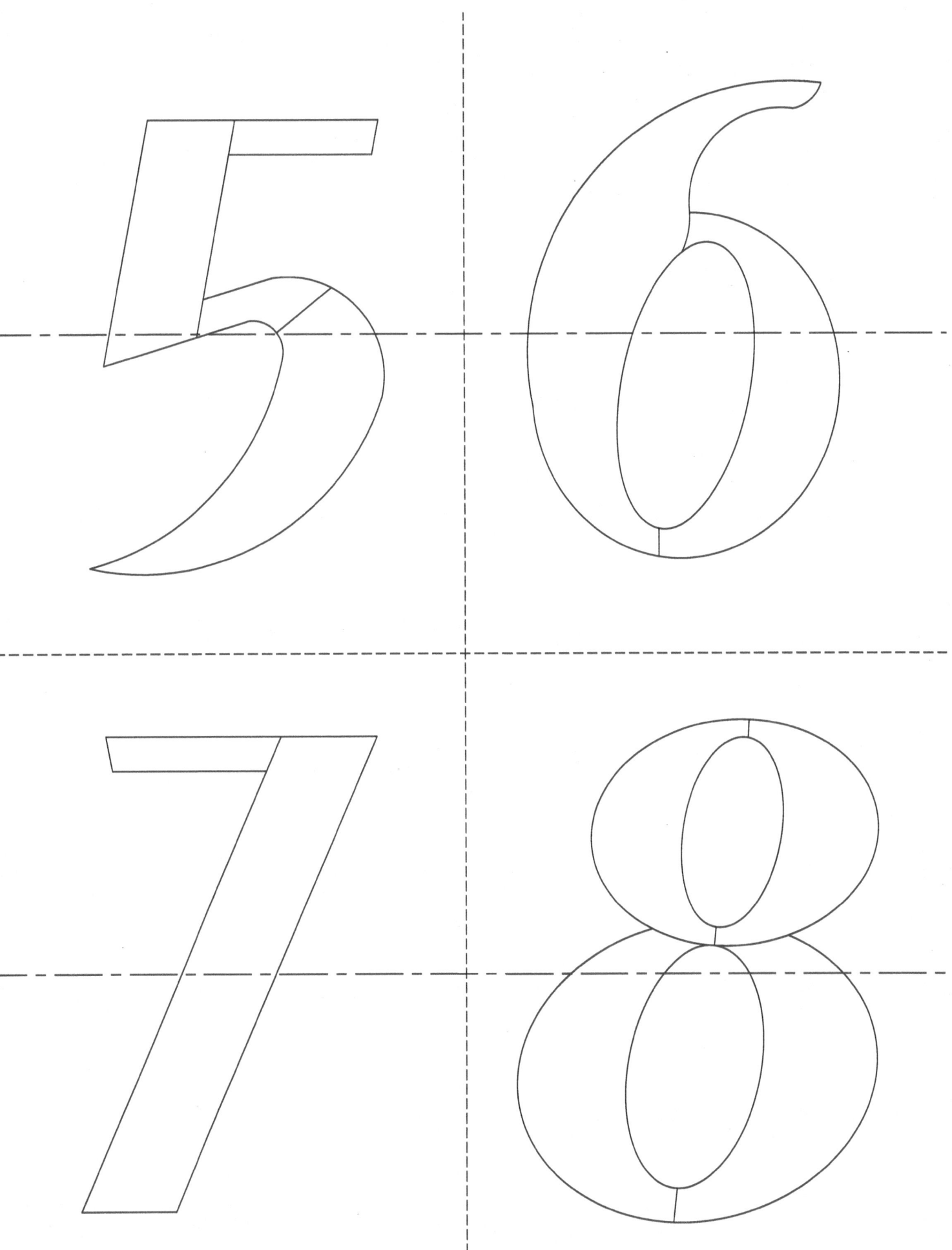

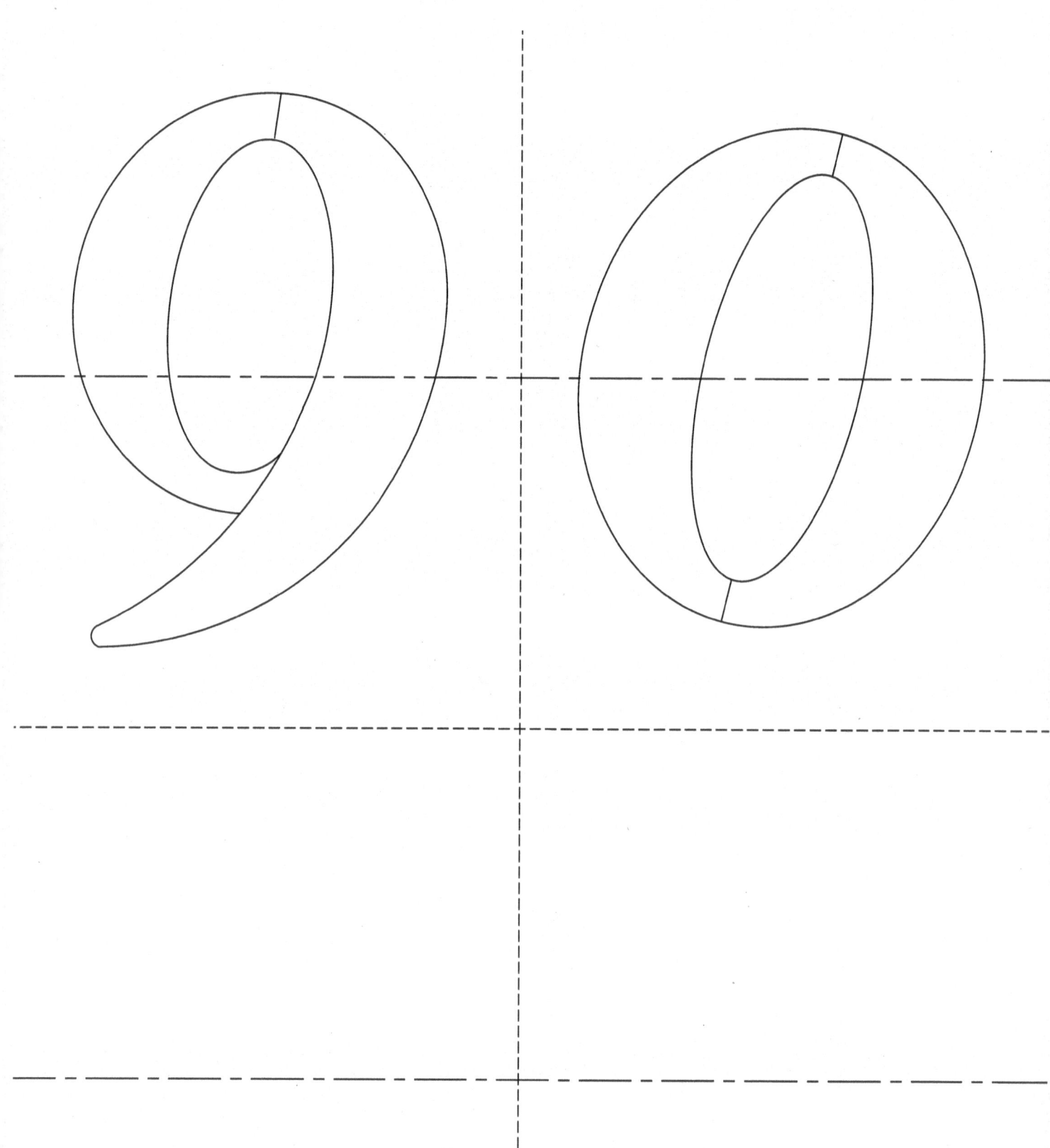

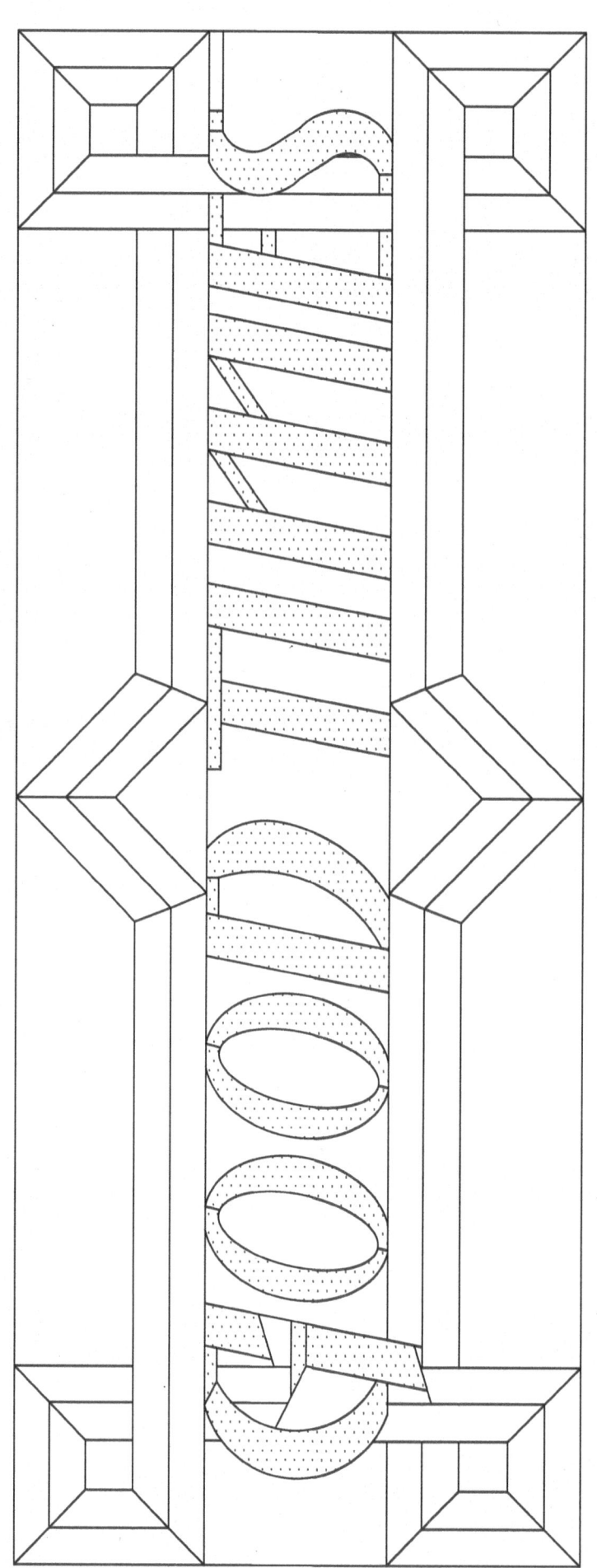

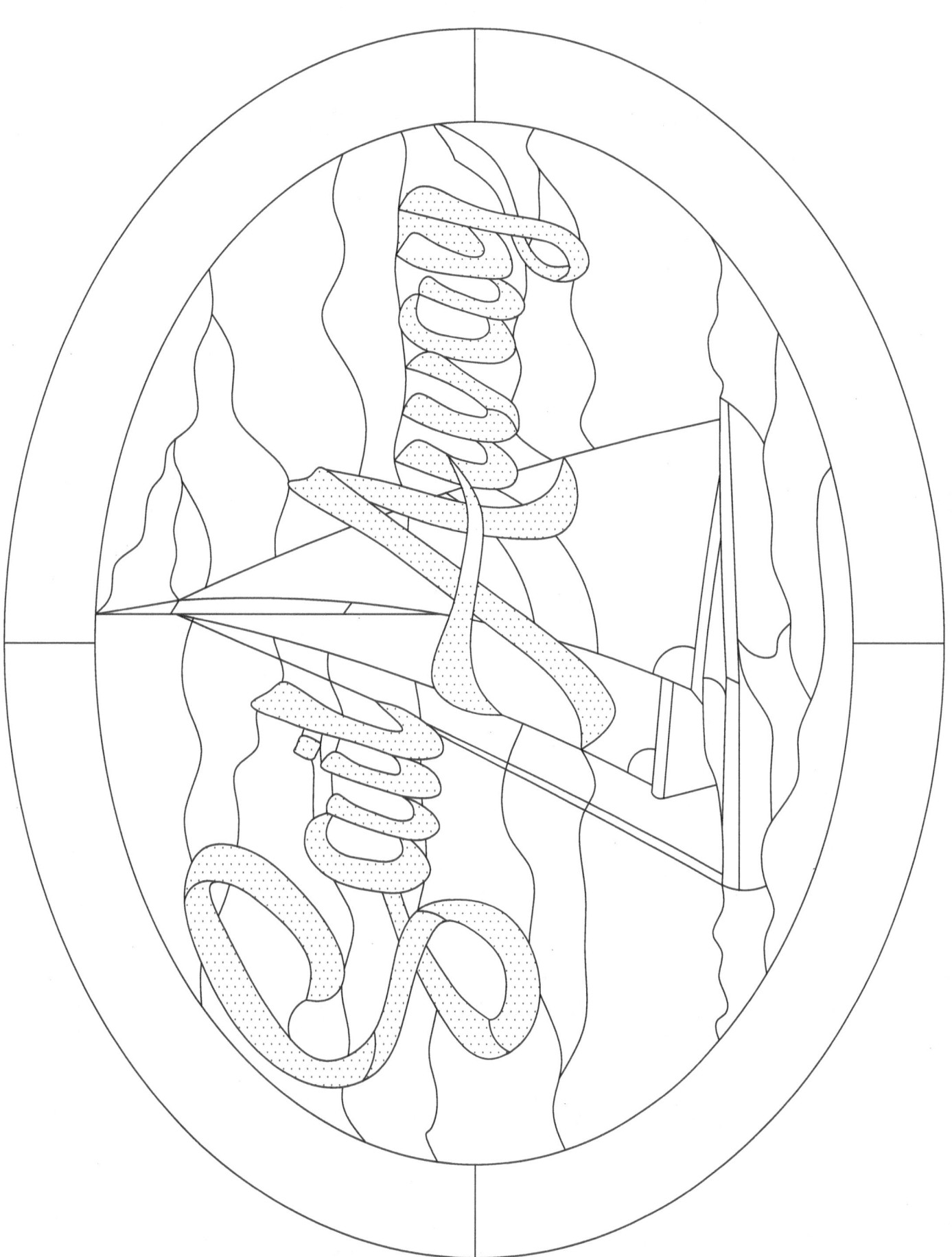

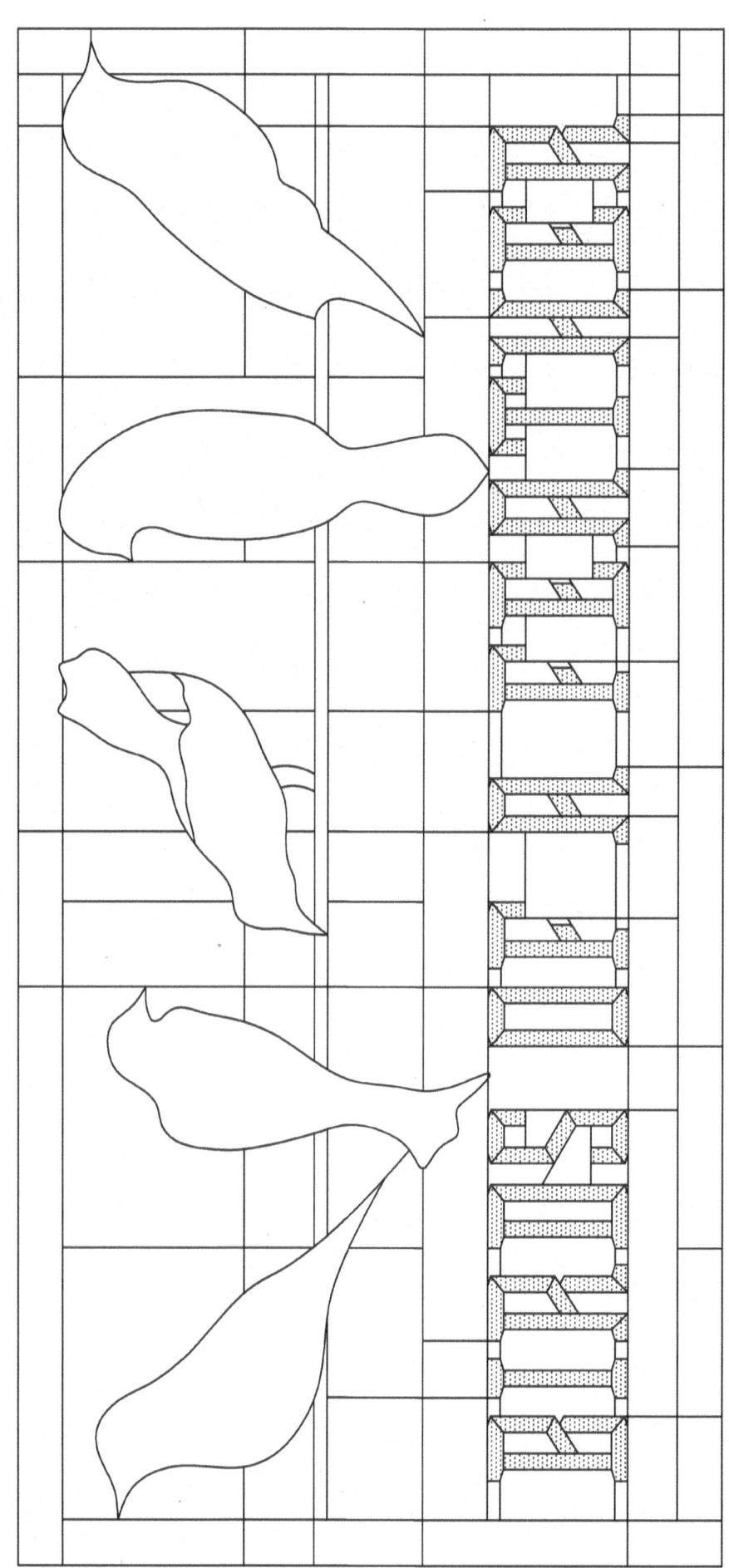

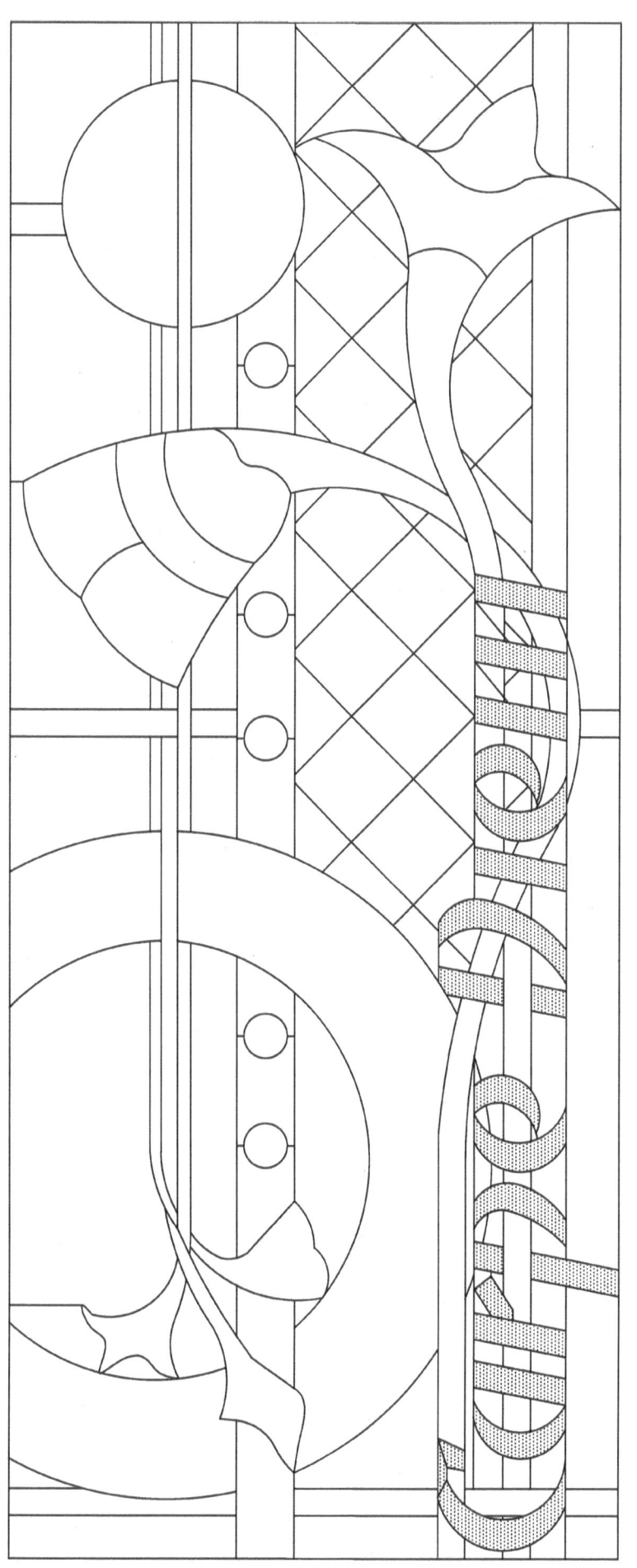

YOUR NAME HERE

TAVERN

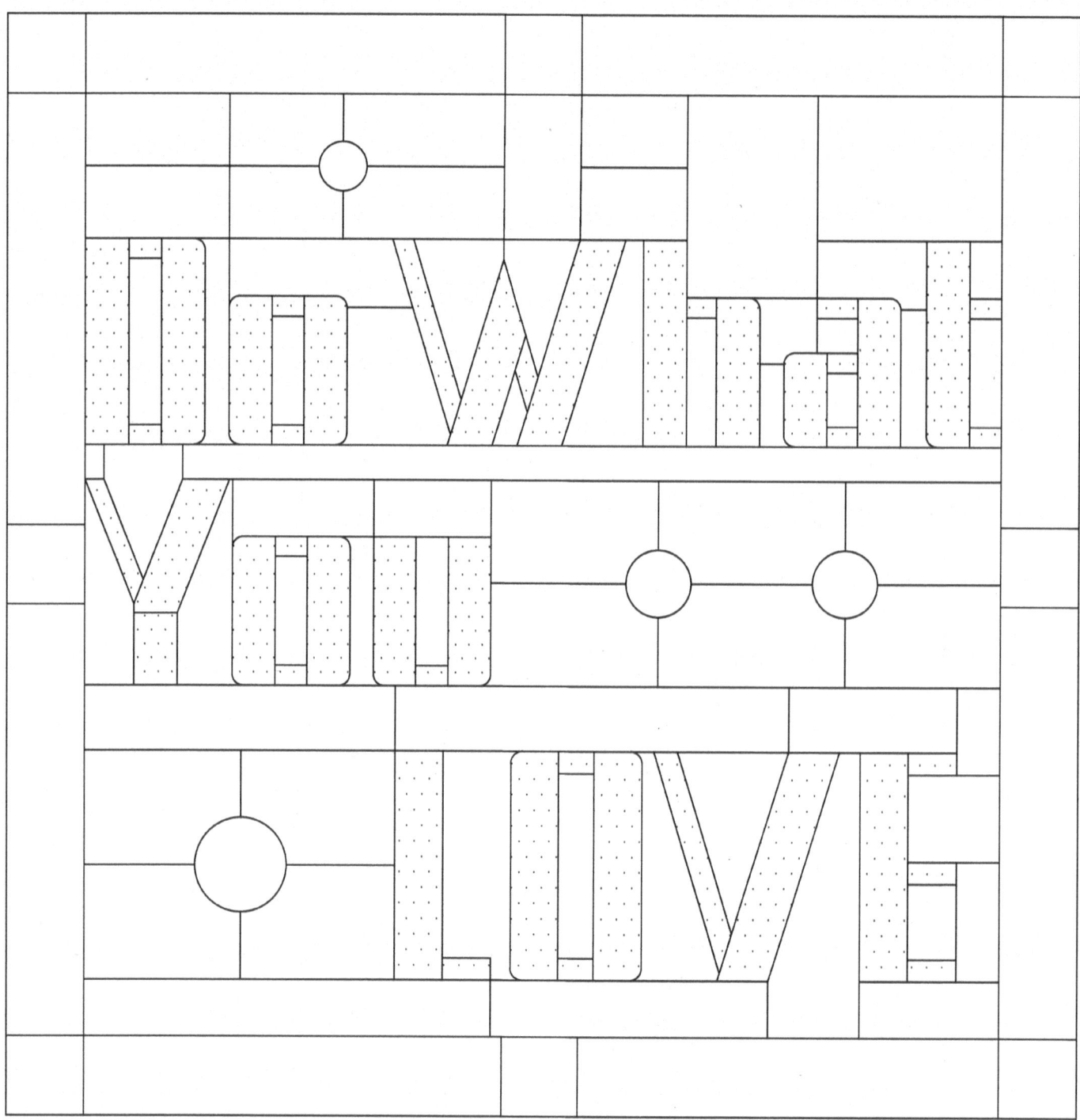

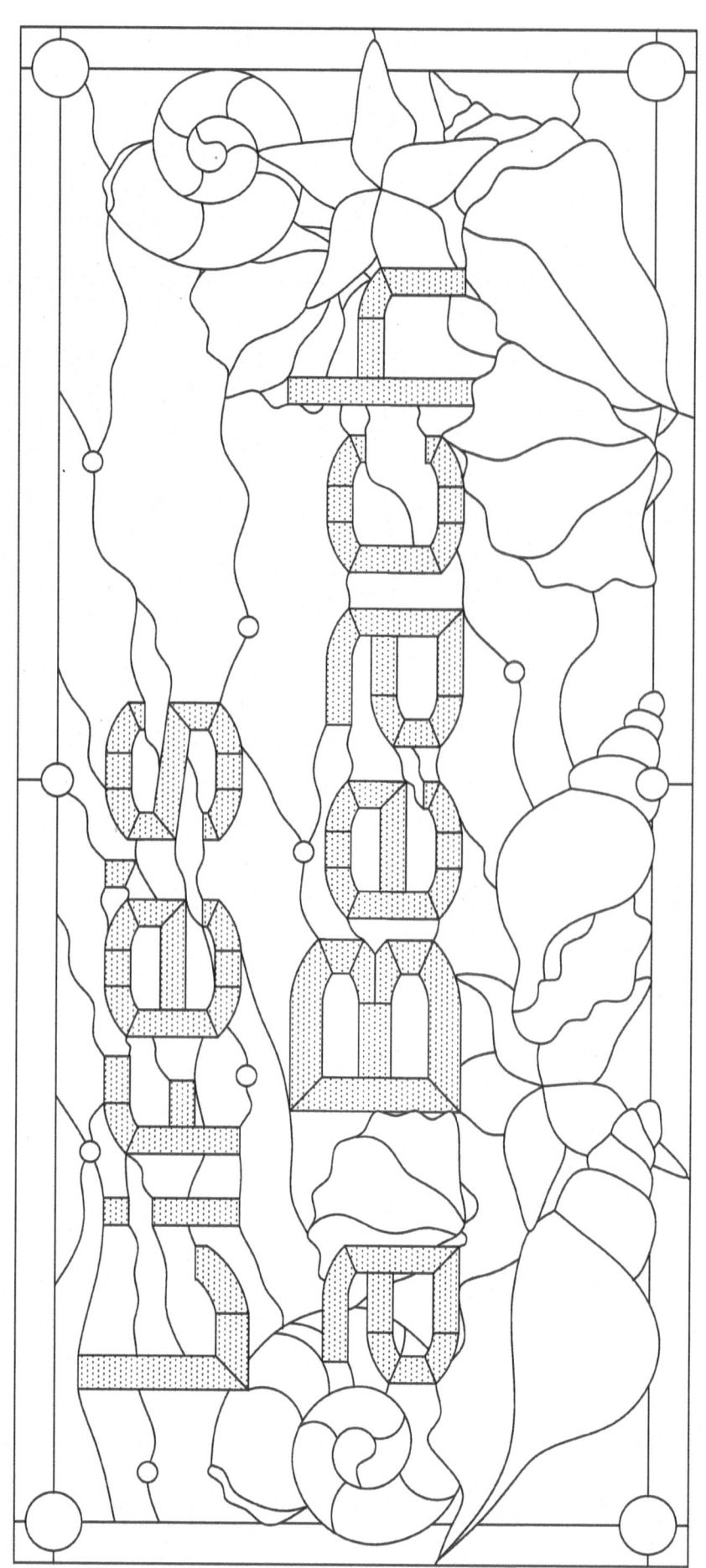

YOUR NAME HERE

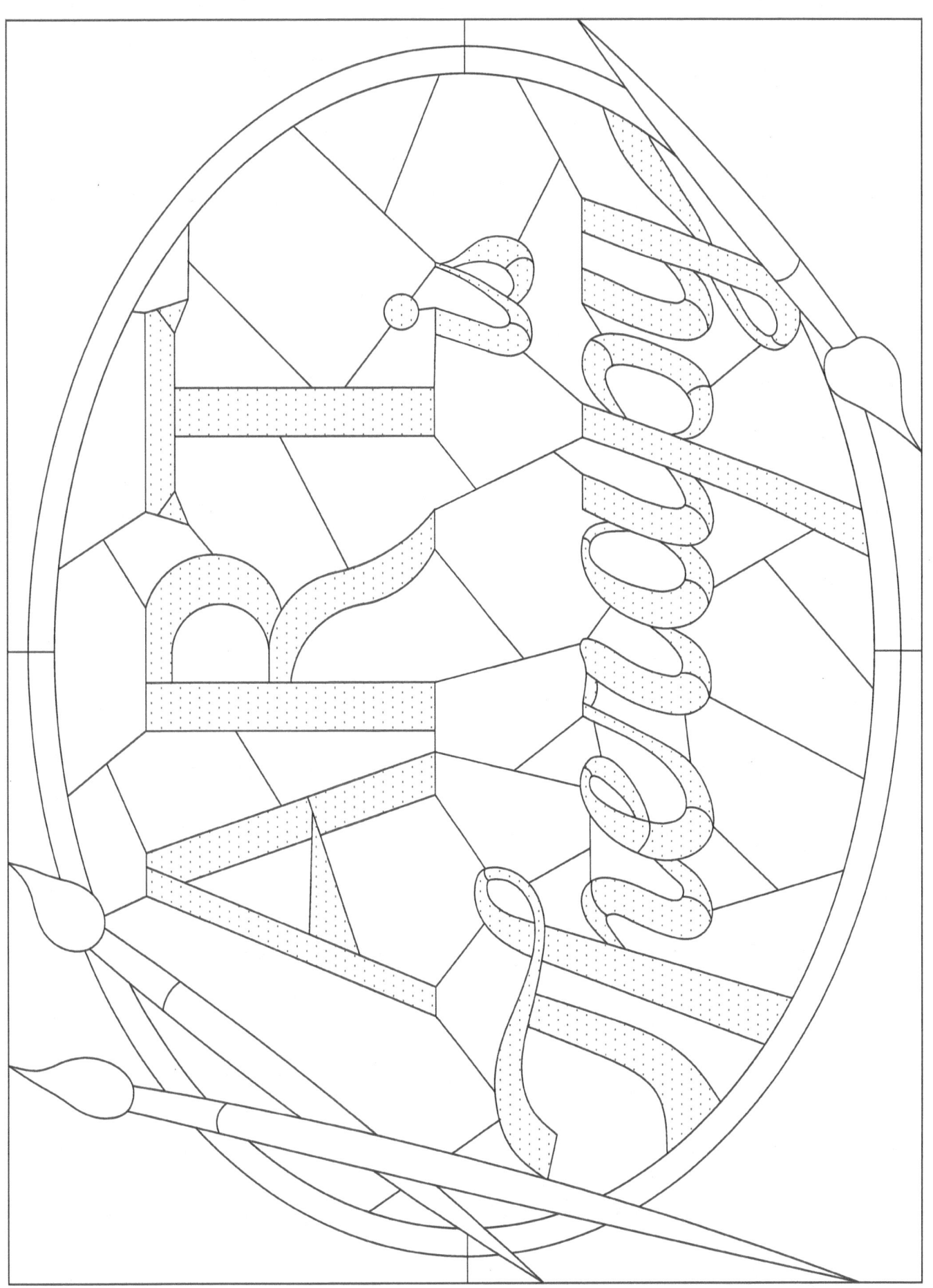